GO-KARTS

Jeff Barger

rourkeeducationalmedia.com

Scan for Related Titles
and Teacher Resources

Before & After Reading Activities

Level: **K**

Teaching Focus:

Have students find capital letters and punctuation in a sentence. Ask students to explain the purpose for using them in a sentence.

Before Reading:

Building Academic Vocabulary and Background Knowledge

Before reading a book, it is important to set the stage for your child or student by using pre-reading strategies. This will help them develop their vocabulary, increase their reading comprehension, and make connections across the curriculum.

1. *Read the title and look at the cover. Let's make predictions about what this book will be about.*
2. *Take a picture walk by talking about the pictures/photographs in the book. Implant the vocabulary as you take the picture walk. Be sure to talk about the text features such as headings, the Table of Contents, glossary, bolded words, captions, charts/diagrams, or index.*
3. *Have students read the first page of text with you then have students read the remaining text.*
4. *Strategy Talk – use to assist students while reading.*
   - *Get your mouth ready*
   - *Look at the picture*
   - *Think…does it make sense*
   - *Think…does it look right*
   - *Think…does it sound right*
   - *Chunk it – by looking for a part you know*
5. *Read it again.*
6. *After reading the book, complete the activities below.*

Content Area Vocabulary

Use glossary words in a sentence.

axle
drum
frame
pedal
rod
transmission

After Reading:

Comprehension and Extension Activity

After reading the book, work on the following questions with your child or students in order to check their level of reading comprehension and content mastery.

1. What is one thing that protects the driver of a go-kart? (Inferring)
2. What is the frame of a go-kart called? (Asking questions)
3. How long can electric go-karts run before they have to be recharged? (Text to self connection)
4. What are the front and rear wheels of a go-kart attached to? (Summarize)

Extension Activity

Think about all the things you read in the book about go-karts. Have you ever ridden a go-kart? Would you like to? If so, what would your go-kart look like? Using a piece of paper and colored pencils, design your own cart. You can make it any color, style, or add different parts to make it your own personal racing machine!

TABLE OF CONTENTS

LET'S GO RACING

Vrooom! Buckle up for a fast ride. Go-karts are built for speed!

Many professional race-car drivers started in go-kart racing.

Go-karts can go up to 160 miles per hour (257 kilometers per hour). That is more than twice as fast as a cheetah.

Go-karts at amusement parks go much slower. Speeds can range from five to 45 miles per hour (eight to 72 kilometers per hour).

Where does the speed come from? How does a go-kart move so fast?

WHAT PUTS THE GO IN GO-KART?

Like your body, a go-kart has several parts.

The **frame** of a go-kart is the chassis.

The first go-kart was built in 1956. It was made from scrap parts and a lawnmower engine.

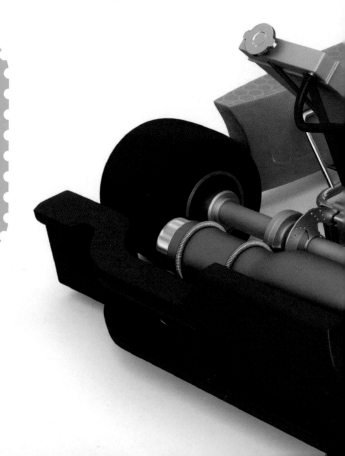

A chassis is like the skeleton, or bones, of a go-kart. It is made of plastic or steel tubes.

chassis

The heart of the go-kart is the engine. Like blood flows through your heart, gasoline flows through an engine.

Electric go-karts can be used for indoor tracks. They will run for about 20 minutes before they need to be recharged.

engine

Air and gas are pulled into the engine.
A spark plug creates a spark causing the air
and gas mixture to explode.

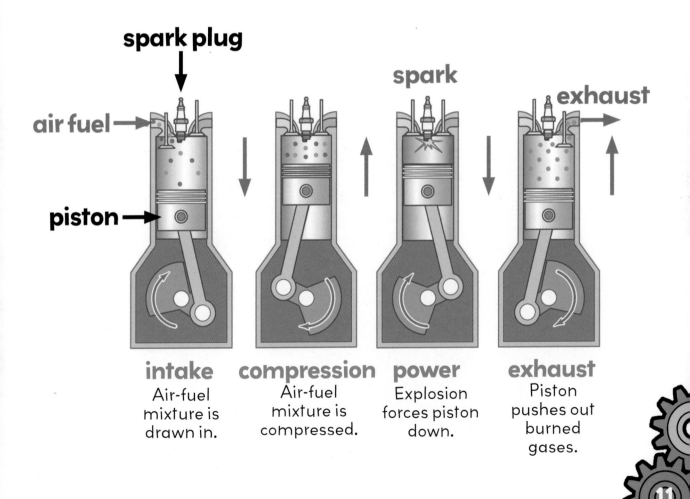

spark plug

spark

exhaust

air fuel →

piston →

intake
Air-fuel
mixture is
drawn in.

compression
Air-fuel
mixture is
compressed.

power
Explosion
forces piston
down.

exhaust
Piston
pushes out
burned
gases.

A **transmission** is the brains of a go-kart. It sends power from the engine to the wheels.

transmission gears

Gears in the transmission harness this power. They allow the go-kart to speed up or slow down.

chain ⟶

gear

gear teeth

STEERING AND BRAKING

Front and rear wheels are attached to the go-kart by a steel **rod** called an **axle.** These rods allow the kart to turn.

The wheel and axle is a simple machine. A simple machine is a basic device that can change the amount or direction of a force.

The steering wheel is connected to the front axle. It lets the driver turn the wheels attached to the axle.

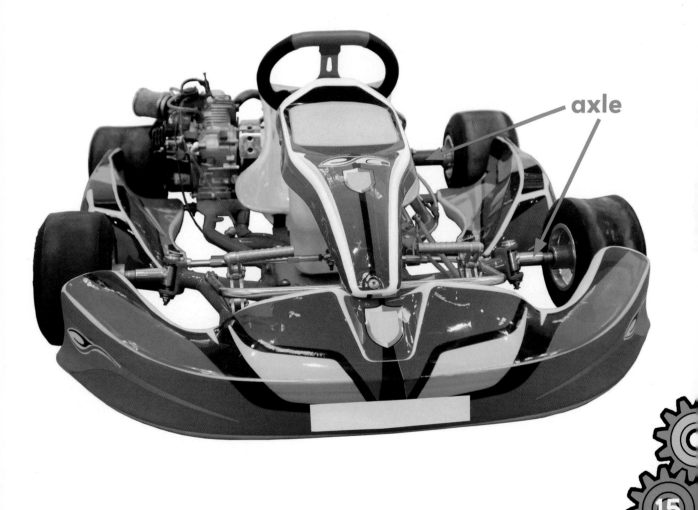

axle

Drivers push on a brake **pedal** to stop a go-kart. The pedal is attached to a long cable.

pedal

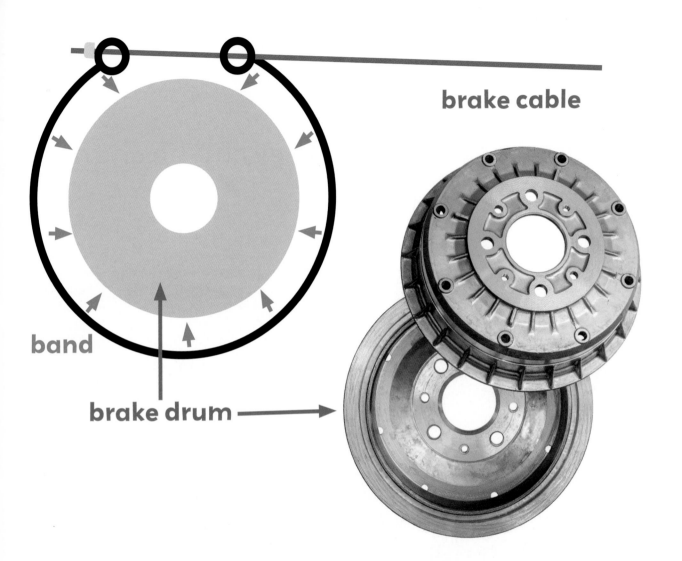

brake cable

band

brake drum →

The cable attaches to a flat band that wraps around a **drum**. Stepping on the pedal stops the drum from turning.

Go-kart tires are small. They can be changed for different conditions.

Wearing a helmet helps protect the driver.

seat belt

Other equipment, such as a seat belt, can be added to a go-kart.

Driving a go-kart is a fun way to learn behind the wheel!

PHOTO GLOSSARY

axle (AK-suhl): A rod in the center of a wheel. The wheel turns around the rod.

drum (druhm): A drum brake uses friction caused by pads that press outward against a rotating cylinder-shaped part called a brake drum.

frame (frame): A basic structure that provides support.

pedal (PED-uhl): A lever that you push with your foot.

rod (rahd): A go-karts wheels are attached to a rod called an axle.

transmission (trans-MISH-uhn): In an automobile, a series of gears that send power from the engine to the wheels.

INDEX

WEBSITES TO VISIT

www.explainthatstuff.com/carengines.html

www.ehow.com/how-does_4565444_a-gocart-work.html

http://wonderopolis.org/wonder/how-does-an-engine-work

ABOUT THE AUTHOR

Jeff Barger is a second grade teacher in North Carolina. He lives with his wife, two daughters, and four pets. Jeff is especially interested in trying to figure out how his beagle's mind works.

Meet The Author!
www.meetREMauthors.com

© 2017 Rourke Educational Media

www.rourkeeducationalmedia.com

PHOTO CREDITS: Cover, p.8-9, p.12-13, 22, 23 ©Fisherman3d; title page, p.21 ©Susan Chiang; p.4 Andreas G. Karelias; p.5 ©Action Sports Photography.; p.6-7 ©Nicky Rhodes; p.10 ©Tatiana Belova; p.11 ©Univeral Images Group North America LLC; p.15 ©Guodingping; p.16, 23 ©Sergei Butorin; p.18 ©fotogaby; p.19 ©Neacsu Razvan Chirnoaga; p.20 ©mg7; p.22 ©Baloncici; p.22 ©Phantom1311; p.23 ©ansonsaw

Edited by: Keli Sipperley

Cover and Interior Design by: Jen Thomas

Library of Congress PCN Data

Go-Karts / Jeff Barger

(How It Works)

ISBN 978-1-68191-685-9 (hard cover)(alk. paper)

ISBN 978-1-68191-786-3 (soft cover)

ISBN 978-1-68191-885-3 (e-Book)

Library of Congress Control Number: 2016932561

Printed in the United States of America, North Mankato, Minnesota

Also Available as: